THE WORLD'S WORST NATURAL DISASTERS

THE WORLD'S WORST EARTHQUAKES

by John R. Baker

CAPSTONE PRESS
a capstone imprint

Blazers Books are published by Capstone Press,
1710 Roe Crest Drive, North Mankato, Minnesota 56003
www.mycapstone.com

Library of Congress Cataloging-in-Publication Data
Names: Baker, John R. (John Ronald), 1989–
Title: The world's worst earthquakes / by John R. Baker.
Description: North Mankato, Minnesota: Capstone Press, 2017. | Series: World's
  worst natural disasters | Audience: Grades 4 to 6. | Includes bibliographical
  references and index. | Description based on print version record and CIP data
  provided by publisher; resource not viewed.
Identifiers: LCCN 2016000443 (print) | LCCN 2015049411 (ebook) | ISBN
  9781515717942 (eBook PDF) | ISBN 9781515717867 (library binding) |
  ISBN 9781515717904 (paperback)
Subjects: LCSH: Earthquakes—History—Juvenile literature.
Classification: LCC QE521.3 (print) | LCC QE521.3 .B33 2017 (ebook) |
  DDC 551.2209—dc23
LC record available at http://lccn.loc.gov/2016000443

Summary: Describes history's biggest and most
  destructive earthquakes from around the world.

Editorial Credits
Aaron Sautter, editor; Steve Mead, designer; Jo Miller,
media researcher; Tori Abraham, production specialist

Photo Credits
Corbis: Sygma/Sergio Dornates, 20–21; Getty Images: AFP/
STF, 8–9, ChinaFotoPress/Yang Weihua, 16-17, Justin Sullivan,
28–29; Glow Images: Stock Connection/View Stock, 10–11;
Newscom: ABACA/DPA, 12–13, akg-images, 24–25, EPA/Sergei
Chirikov, 22–23, Reuters/Damir Sagolj, 26–27; Shutterstock:
leonello calvetti, cover, 3, 31, think4photop, cover, Tom Wang,
4–5; Wikimedia: NARA/Chadwick, H.D., 14–15, UN Photo/
Logan Abassi, 6–7, US Navy/PH2 Philip A. McDaniel, 18–19

Design Elements
Shutterstock: SDubi, xpixel

TABLE OF CONTENTS

EARTH-SHAKING POWER

THE RICHTER SCALE

9.0+
8.0
7.0
6.0
5.0
4.0
3.0
2.0
0.0

The **magnitude** of earthquakes is measured using the Richter scale. Weak earthquakes have a lower magnitude. Powerful earthquakes are rated at a 7.0 or higher.

magnitude—a measure of the size of an earthquake

The ground rumbles and splits open. Bridges sway. Buildings topple. What's causing this destruction? An **earthquake**! These powerful ground-shaking events occur somewhere on Earth nearly every hour. Grab on tight. It's time to learn about the worst earthquakes in the world.

MAGNITUDE

0.0–1.9	2.0–2.9	3.0–3.9	4.0–4.9	5.0–5.9	6.0–6.9	7.0–7.9	8.0–8.9	9.0+
detectable only by special instruments	barely detectable	felt indoors	slight damage	minor damage	moderate destruction	serious destruction	devastating destruction	near total destruction

Effects

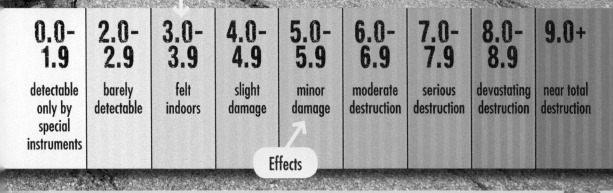

earthquake—a sudden shaking of the ground when the earth's crust shifts

DISASTER IN HAITI

#2

Location:
Port-au-Prince,
Haiti

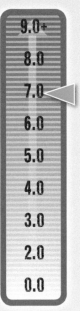

Date:
January 12, 2010

Rating:

9.0+
8.0
7.0
6.0
5.0
4.0
3.0
2.0
0.0

Haiti wasn't prepared for the major 7.0 earthquake that struck in 2010. The quake's **epicenter** was close to the city of Port-au-Prince. Thousands of buildings collapsed. More than 200,000 people died in the disaster.

Hundreds of thousands of people were left homeless after the Haiti earthquake. Many of the survivors were forced to live in tents.

epicenter—the point on Earth's surface directly above the place where an earthquake occurs

TOPPING THE SCALE

Location:
Chile

Date:
May 22, 1960

Rating:

9.0+
8.0
7.0
6.0
5.0
4.0
3.0
2.0
0.0

On May 22, 1960, the strongest earthquake in history hit Chile. The quake measured an incredible 9.5 magnitude on the Richter scale. Three destructive **tsunamis** then slammed into Chile's coast. The disaster killed about 1,600 people.

About 16
earthquakes with
a magnitude of 7.0
or greater occur
around the world
each year.

tsunami—a large, destructive ocean wave caused by an underwater
earthquake, landslide, or volcanic eruption

HISTORY'S DEADLIEST QUAKE

Location:
Shaanxi
(Shensi), China

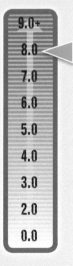

Date:
January 23, 1556

Rating:

9.0+
8.0
7.0
6.0
5.0
4.0
3.0
2.0
0.0

The deadliest known earthquake occurred in China on January 23, 1556. The killer 8.0 quake claimed the lives of more than 830,000 people. The huge earthquake also changed the land. Mountains crumbled. The paths of rivers changed. Major floods hit many areas.

Experts believe **liquefaction** caused much of the destruction in the 1556 earthquake. The quake caused loose soil under buildings to flow like a liquid. Buildings then toppled without sturdy ground under them.

liquefaction—the process of soil becoming fluidlike and unstable during an earthquake

NEPAL TRAGEDY

Location:
Nepal

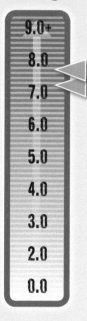

Date:
April 25 and
May 12, 2015

Rating:

9.0+
8.0
7.0
6.0
5.0
4.0
3.0
2.0
0.0

On April 25, 2015, a 7.8 earthquake rocked Nepal. A 7.3-magnitude **aftershock** shook the area several days later. **Landslides** flattened entire villages. About 9,000 people died in the disaster. Hundreds of thousands more lost their homes.

aftershock—a smaller earthquake that follows a large one
landslide—a large mass of earth and rocks that suddenly slides down a mountain or hill

12

The first Nepal earthquake shifted Mount Everest, the world's tallest mountain. It moved about 1.2 inches (3 centimeters) southwest.

SAN FRANCISCO DISASTER

Location:
San Francisco, California

Date:
April 18, 1906

Rating:

9.0+
8.0
7.0
6.0
5.0
4.0
3.0
2.0
0.0

A powerful 7.8 earthquake shook San Francisco in 1906. It crumbled houses and burst water mains. When fires broke out, firefighters didn't have enough water. The fires burned for two days. About 3,000 people died in the disaster.

San Francisco lies near the San Andreas **Fault**. In the 1906 earthquake, a fence on the fault broke in two. The two ends shifted about 15 feet (5 meters) apart.

fault—a crack in the earth's crust; earthquakes often occur along faults

CHINESE LANDSLIDES

Location:
Sichuan province,
China

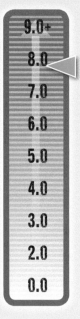

Date:
May 12, 2008

Rating:

9.0+
8.0
7.0
6.0
5.0
4.0
3.0
2.0
0.0

China is home to many earthquakes. A 7.9-magnitude quake hit Sichuan **province** on May 12, 2008. More than 87,000 people died or went missing. Large landslides blocked the narrow mountain roads. The army sent helicopters to rescue survivors.

FACT

The landslides also blocked some rivers. Many lakes were formed. The largest threatened the homes of more than 1 million people. The government blasted through tons of rock to release the water.

province—a district or a region of some countries

RECORD QUAKE IN INDONESIA

Location:
Sumatra, Indonesia

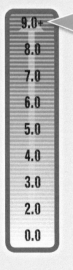

Date:
December 26, 2004

Rating:

9.0+
8.0
7.0
6.0
5.0
4.0
3.0
2.0
0.0

On December 26, 2004, a massive 9.1 earthquake hit near the coast of Sumatra, Indonesia. It created one of the deadliest tsunamis ever recorded. The killer wave reached up to 100 feet (30 m) high. More than 220,000 people died or went missing.

FACT

The 2004 Sumatra earthquake was the third-strongest ever recorded. It created a 900-mile (1,500-kilometer) long crack on the ocean floor.

ON SHAKY GROUND

A powerful 8.0 earthquake hit near Mexico City on September 19, 1985. The city's soft ground made the disaster worse. The quake's **seismic waves** easily toppled unsteady buildings. The disaster killed at least 9,500 people.

FACT

After the earthquake Mexico's government passed laws to make sure new buildings were stronger.

TERROR IN TURKEY

Location:
Izmit, Turkey

Date:
August 17, 1999

Rating:

- 9.0+
- 8.0
- 7.0
- 6.0
- 5.0
- 4.0
- 3.0
- 2.0
- 0.0

People in Izmit, Turkey, got a horrible shock on August 17, 1999. A 7.6-magnitude earthquake shook them awake in the middle of the night. Many buildings collapsed. The disaster killed at least 17,000 people. It injured another 50,000.

FACT

About 500,000 people in Turkey lost their homes in the 1999 earthquake.

GOOD FRIDAY EARTHQUAKE

Location:
Prince William
Sound, Alaska

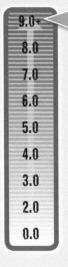

Date:
March 27, 1964

Rating:

9.0+
8.0
7.0
6.0
5.0
4.0
3.0
2.0
0.0

The Alaskan earthquake caused a giant tsunami. The huge wave reached as far as Hawaii. It claimed 113 lives.

The second-strongest earthquake ever recorded hit in 1964. On Good Friday, the 9.2 quake shook towns along Alaska's coast. Docks fell into the sea. Railroad tracks were bent and twisted. Many buildings collapsed. Incredibly, only 15 people in Alaska died.

JAPANESE DISASTERS

Location:
Japan

Date:
March 11, 2011

Rating:

9.0+
8.0
7.0
6.0
5.0
4.0
3.0
2.0
0.0

March 11, 2011, was a terrible day in Japan. A massive 9.0-magnitude earthquake triggered a huge, 100-foot (30-m) high tsunami. The giant wave then flooded a nuclear power plant. It caused a **meltdown**. The disasters killed more than 15,000 people.

FACT Japan is no stranger to earthquakes. In 1923 a magnitude 7.9 quake struck just south of Tokyo. It triggered fires that quickly spread. The quake and fires killed more than 140,000 people.

meltdown—an accident in a nuclear reactor in which the fuel overheats and melts the reactor core or shielding

SURVIVING AN EARTHQUAKE

It's important to know what to do if an earthquake hits. If you're indoors, take shelter under a desk or other strong piece of furniture. If you're outside, move away from buildings. They could collapse as you run into them. Stay calm. Try to think clearly. Acting smart will help keep you safe.

DISASTER EMERGENCY KIT

An emergency kit can be very helpful in case of an earthquake. A good kit should include these items:

- ✔ first-aid kit
- ✔ flashlight
- ✔ battery-powered radio
- ✔ extra batteries
- ✔ blankets
- ✔ bottled water
- ✔ canned and dried food
- ✔ can opener
- ✔ whistle to alert rescue workers

GLOSSARY

aftershock (AF-tur-shok)—a smaller earthquake that follows a large one

earthquake (UHRTH-kwayk)—a sudden shaking of the ground when the earth's crust shifts

epicenter (EP-uh-sent-ur)—the point on Earth's surface directly above the place where an earthquake occurs

fault (FAWLT)—a crack in the earth's crust; earthquakes often occur along faults

landslide (LAND-slyd)—a large mass of earth and rocks that suddenly slides down a mountain or hill

liquefaction (lik-wuh-FAK-shuhn)—the process of soil becoming fluidlike and unstable during an earthquake

magnitude (MAG-nuh-tood)—a measure of the size of an earthquake

meltdown (MELT-down)—an accident in a nuclear reactor in which the fuel overheats and melts the reactor core or shielding

province (PROV-inss)—a district or a region of some countries

seismic wave (SIZE-mik WAYV)—movement in the ground created by an earthquake

tsunami (tsoo-NAH-mee)—a large, destructive ocean wave caused by an underwater earthquake, landslide, or volcanic eruption

READ MORE

Burgan, Michael. *Surviving Earthquakes.* Children's True Stories: Natural Disasters. Chicago: Raintree, 2012.

Collins, Terry. *Buried in Rubble: True Tales of Surviving Earthquakes.* True Stories of Survival. North Mankato, Minn.: Capstone Press, 2016.

Ganeri, Anita. *Fearsome Forces of Nature.* Extreme Nature. Chicago: Raintree, 2013.

INTERNET SITES

Facthound offers a safe, fun way to find Internet sites related to this book. All of the sites on Facthound have been researched by our staff.

Here's all you do:
Visit *www.facthound.com*
Type in this code: 9781515717867

Check out projects, games and lots more at
www.capstonekids.com

CRITICAL THINKING USING THE COMMON CORE

1. Earthquakes are some of the most powerful natural disasters in the world. Which earthquake was the strongest ever recorded? Which one killed the most people in history? (Key Ideas and Details)

2. Explain what you should do if an earthquake occurs in your area. (Craft and Structure)

3. Look at the chart on pages 4–5. What kind of damage can be expected for each level of magnitude on the Richter scale? (Integration of Knowledge and Ideas)

INDEX